HOW TO GIVE HIM AN INCREDIBLE HANDJOB

IN DEPTH HANDJOB TIPS THAT WILL CAUSE HIM TO ERUPT IN BED

BARRY MORGAN

DEDICATION

To All Women That Desire To Satisfy Their Men
Sexually

CONTENTS

1 Introduction 1

2 Why Men Love Handjob 10

3 Amazing Handjob Ideas And Techniques 17

4 Common Handjob Mistakes Women Make 50

5 Frequently Asked Questions About Handjobs 56

CHAPTER 1

INTRODUCTION

Oral sex and foreplay is often a very essential part of sex. But while there is a lot of information out there telling men how to pleasure women, there isn't enough telling women what men actually like when it comes to handjobs (when you help a man orgasm with your hands).

A handjob is any stimulation from the hand of a partner on (another person's) typically in a fashion that simulates the thrusting of penetrative sex. So while there are lots of different ways to stimulate the penis, the giver moving their hand up and down — from the base of the shaft to the head, or glans, of the receiver's penis — is what's typically understood by the term "handjob."

If there's a single sex act most associated with being a teenager, it's undoubtedly the infamous handjob. More intimate than French kissing or heavy petting, manual stimulation of the genitals — by another person, specifically — crosses a clear boundary from sensual into sexual.

At the same time, it's a sex act that many people leave behind, intentionally or otherwise, when they begin engaging in oral sex, anal or vaginal penetrative sex. Compared to those heavy hitters, handjobs can be seen as less impressive, less desirable, less special, or even less sexy.

For guys who are on the prowl for sex, a handjob can seem boring. After all, as he's likely used to touching his own penis with his own hands, someone else's hand might not seem that special when considering the sensation of a mouth, vagina or anus.

But is it really fair to consider the handjob somehow lesser form of sex? Handjobs get a bad rap for being 'not real' sex or simply not as sexy. For many people, a handjob is something you did as a teenager to pretend you weren't having sex (you totally were) while also not fearing pregnancy or STIs.As a result, some people truly don't enjoy giving a handjob, because it's seen as the 'least sexy' option.

Guys who demand handjobs when their partner won't provide oral or penetrative sex haven't helped either. Sulking or pouting because you're getting the 'not as good' version doesn't exactly cement the act as a favorite one in people's minds.The poor, mistreated handjob doesn't really deserve that reputation.

Not to mention, handjobs have an erotic aspect to them

that's underappreciated, too. Handjobs can be slow and sensual, a 'cruel' tease to turn a partner on and then make him wait.

And yet, handjobs are incredibly versatile. They can be performed by almost anyone — all you need is a person with a penis and a person with a hand. They can be performed almost anywhere in any position, whether sitting, standing, lying down, or even underwater. They can be paired with mutual masturbation (both giving and providing manual stimulation at the same time). They're the sneaky thing you can do in public to be kinky or sexy that you're least likely to get caught doing. And handjobs are easier and safer than blowjobs while driving. A hand job is as sexy, intimate or kinky as you make it.

They can take under a minute to complete, but can be stretched out for hours if you're really going for it. And unlike oral and penetrative sex, they don't require any safe-sex protection as they won't lead to STI transmission or pregnancy. In short, there's a lot to like about handjobs.

When was the last time you intentionally set aside time to give your partner a handjob outside of a foreplay scenario? Folks in the sex ed industry often joke that our hands are the most versatile "sex organ" on the human body, given that (unlike the genitals) we can move them into any shape or configuration and acutely control how much pressure we're applying with them.

Plus, since hand sex cannot get someone pregnant, and it's extremely difficult to transmit an STI from the genitals to the hands (and vice versa), it's surprising that handjob is often glossed over as being an adolescent sex act, or something that ought to remain within the realm of foreplay. (This likely has a lot to do with the mainstream's penetration and penis-in-vagina intercourse-centric attitude towards human sexuality).

But here's the thing: While handjobs make having safer sex a breeze, they can also be incredibly hot. Of course, handjobs do make for amazing foreplay, but they're also a great way to continue pleasuring your partner if you've come and/or are exhausted. Not to mention, giving a handjob can be an exciting, discreet way to get your partner off in a car, bathroom, or any other cramped space outside the bedroom. Also, if you're particularly vulnerable to infections, or simply have a more sensitive body, handjobs are a great way to give your body a break if you need a moment of rest but still want to pleasure your partner.

You may be good at giving him head, but as many men

would dare to tell you, they would like you to know how to possibly give a good hand job the right way too. The two go together like sugar and spice to make something more than just nice – a mind-blowing experience!

Still not convinced? Well, let's crunch some numbers: the average penis is 5 to 6 inches in length, while the average mouth is only 2 to 3 inches deep. And unless you're that talented in deep throat, your hands can make up for the difference to ensure that your man gets the total workout.

Besides that, giving a good hand job is a great way if you want to do something naughty for your partner but don't want to get a dick in your mouth, especially when you're just hooking up and you don't know his past.

Being generous sexually is crucial for a lasting relationship You don't always enjoy giving this. Truth be told, a hand job – no matter how quick or slow – just doesn't do much for women. It can even be boring. However, it's still something very nice and generous to do for your partner. And giving him something special even if you don't get anything in return is important.

You need to be able to give your lover what he needs in a relationship – and vice versa. Giving is a huge part of what makes good sex, and good sex is one of the reasons relationships last. If both of you are always making sure the other gets little surprises now and then, your relationship will be much healthier.

Ready to learn how to give a handjob that he'll never forget? First, forget everything you think you know about handjobs. Forget the image of holding on and pumping up and down in the same frenzied motion over and over again. We're not quite sure when this one-stroke model for touching men became the norm, but throw it out the window – men deserve a lot more finesse than that. Touch your man with creativity and curiosity, and use your hands to create the widest range of sensation possible.

If you want to see him moaning with pleasure, you need to know how to give a great hand job that will blow his mind. Use these hand job tips in this book to drive him crazy. If you think intercourse is the only way to have sex, let these handjob tips remind you that outercourse is also a really dope way to have sex.

CHAPTER 2

WHY MEN LOVE HANDJOB

The humble handjob doesn't always get a good press. A lot of women are nervous about giving them, they lack the cultural cache of their oral counterpart, and they're rarely more than an afterthought in most mainstream sex columns, overshadowed in glitz and erotic glamour by the latest in an endless line of new kinks on the block.

Needless to say, I love them. Hand jobs are awesome – just not for the reasons you think they're awesome. We'll come to that a bit later.

First, it's worth thinking about why they're underappreciated – and why so many women are super-confident when it comes to blow jobs, but strangely hesitant about hand jobs.

The answer to that lies in one fundamental truth: we can do the second of those better than you.Of course we can. After all, using our hands to get off is something most of us guys have been doing day-in, day-out since our mid-teens.

We've spent literally thousands of hours at it, and if the main thought going through your head as you curl your fingers round it is 'I won't be able to do this as well as he can do it himself', the chances are you're probably right.

And at the same time so, so wrong.

Here's the thing: maybe you can't make us come as quickly as we could do it ourselves, maybe you don't know just how much pressure we like, or what to do with your thumb, or how much time you should spend focusing on the head.

Even after we've told you those things, you might not be able to grip as firmly as we can, or develop that instinctive feel for when to speed up or slow down – or when to keep going at exactly the same speed.

But so what?

I can say with relative certainty that every partner I've had has known her vagina better than I have. I can read body language, I can fall back on experience, and I can respond to guidance, but I will never be able to feel the effect my actions are having, so there will always be tiny missteps. Moments when the rhythm is great – but not quite perfect. 95% there, 98% even. Just not perfect.

Every now and then, I'll give an A+ hand job, exactly how she'd have done it herself. But even with a partner I know well, it won't happen every time. Not because I'm bad at it, or because I don't listen to her, but because it simply can't.

Still, lots of women love being fingered, for any one of a hundred reasons. Nostalgia. The power dynamic. The prioritisation of their pleasure. How easy it is to do it in public, or somewhere you really shouldn't. Just the basic care and attention it involves.

There's a physical side to it too.

In most cases, my fingers are longer and thicker than my partner's. I'm stronger, so I can thrust and pump more vigorously. I can do it from different angles.

Either way, it's not a proxy for something they could do themselves, and the appeal goes beyond basic clitoral or vaginal stimulation. There's a wider context, which is often where the hotness comes from.

The same is true of hand jobs.

As guys, we don't expect – or even want – you to touch our cocks in exactly the same way we do it ourselves. It's not that we're too lazy to masturbate, and we don't see the end goal of your endeavours as an efficient, fault-free orgasm, complete with perfect dismount and landing.

We love hand jobs – or I love hand jobs – because of everything that goes with them. It's that wider context again.

• I love that my partner wants to touch me, and to give me pleasure.

• I love feeling her explore my cock with her lubed-up hand, discovering all the different ways of playing with it.

• I love that she'll do things to it that I wouldn't have done myself, but in a really good, surprising way.

• I love the way she talks dirty to me – or maybe how she stays completely silent, focused only on my breathing.

• I love that every now and then her other hand will wander down to touch herself – that it gets her horny too.

• I love the delight on her face when I come. The sense of achievement and the joy of watching me have an orgasm.

• I love the power dynamics and the way she can use her hand to control me – to edge me closer to the orgasm I really want, but can't have.

it's not about the mechanics. Yes, there are things a woman shouldn't do – I don't want to feel like I've got my cock caught in a mechanical vice, for example, nor do I want her to try and pull it off my body – but it's up to me to tell her, or better yet to show her.

I have 20 years' experience of making myself come, and

unsurprisingly I'm damn good at it.If all you want to do is replicate how your partner masturbates, you are probably going to fail.

However, once you realise that there's so much more to a hand job than its basic parts – that honestly, sometimes we just want to be touched – it becomes one of the absolute best things you can do to, for, or with a man. Trust me on this one.

CHAPTER 3

AMAZING HANDJOB IDEAS AND TECHNIQUES

Learning how to give a great hand job to your man is a valuable weapon to have in your sex toolbox, along with learning how to give a good blow job. That's why I'm giving you different hand job techniques below that will bring your man back-arching ecstasy and having him begging you for more.

Now, you may be wondering what the best handjob technique is. The truth is there is no perfect, works-on-every-guy hand job technique. This is crucial to understand. The truth is different guys like different things. So if you think that one hand job tip will work every time on every guy, then you are mistaken.

Fortunately, this book will teach you enough different

hand job ideas, techniques, and tips so you will always have something for your man to enjoy.

Before we get to my famous hand job techniques, we're first going to cover a CRUCIAL aspect of hand jobs that is often overlooked.

1. Your Hands

Of course, the most important part of learning how to give a good hand job is your hands. Rough, calloused hands aren't going to make for a particularly satisfying hand job and can even make it painful (unless your man likes rough sex). So before you even get to giving your man a handjob, make sure your hands are soft and smooth so that they provide maximum pleasure.

Here's a quick checklist of things you should probably do beforehand if your hands aren't in good shape:

• Use a pumice stone on tough callouses.

• Keep your hands moisturized, so they stay soft.

• Keep your nails free of sharp edges that may hurt him.

• Keep them clean.

2. The Build Up...Or No Build Up

Many women adore a slow build up towards sex. Sexual tension, slowly amped up throughout an evening, day or even whole week, followed by teasing foreplay before reaching a climax of lust and passion can be incredibly satisfying and even addictive.

Many men also enjoy this build up and being teased into a sexual frenzy. But others find that a long build with sexual tension and foreplay before sex can be frustrating and even a turn off. They hate it.

So keep this in mind for your man. If he doesn't enjoy

foreplay and prefers getting right down to it, then scroll down to the next technique.

If he does enjoy it, then before you even take his penis out of his trousers, try slowly and gently massaging his penis outside his pants. This is probably the easiest thing you can do to turn him on and arouse him. You just need to use your hand(s) to massage his inner thighs, his testicles and his penis outside his trousers. It's that simple!

You'll find that you can also use your fingers to slowly 'tickle' his balls and penis while doing this.

You can use this technique for as little as a minute before you start giving him a hand job. But, you can also do it for much longer if you are sitting down on the sofa watching TV or just lying in bed together.

3. Reach Inside With Gentle Fingers

After rubbing your man outside his trousers for a while, you will then want to move inside. You will need to unzip his trousers and pull them down along with his briefs too.

You may be eager to start giving him a hand job the minute you see his penis, but at this stage, it's still a good idea to keep teasing him and building anticipation. So, instead of just grabbing his penis and starting to give him a hand job, move your fingertips gently over it.

Make sure to keep your touch super light and soft as you trail your fingers up and down his penis. Try touching him like this as far down as his perineum (the patch of rough skin between his testicles and anus) all the way to the head of his penis, aka the glans.

Side note: Use these tips to make him hard if he isn't already.

4. Pre-cum Play

If he is already pre-cumming at this stage, touch it with a fingertip and then slowly trace your fingertip around the head of his penis spreading his precum across it.

His precum is the perfect lube, so it will make the sensations from your fingertips even more intense. The longer you build up to foreplay, the more likely your man will start producing precum. So, don't be surprised by a lack of precum if you suddenly launch into giving him a hand job.

5. The Gentle Claw

Another very sensual handjob technique is to make your fingers into a sort of claw, just like the ones you find in those games in bowling alleys and games arcades where you try to position the claw and then pick up a prize, usually a teddy bear or stuffed animal.

This time you'll be keeping your fingertips together as you lower your hand onto the head of his penis. Your fingertips will touch it first. Then allow your fingertips to spread out over the head of his penis as you lower it further down.

You can focus everything on the head of his penis, or you can move your fingers further down to his shaft too.

Simply moving your hand up and down with a minimal amount of pressure will provide him with lots of sensations, especially if you are using lube. Of course, you can change things up too, by varying the amount of pressure you apply.

This is also something you can try when giving your man a lingam massage.

6. Traditional With A Twist

The 'standard' or traditional way to give your man a hand job is to grab his penis and wrap your fingers around it and then stroke it up and down. It's easy, but it's slightly dull.

Thankfully there is an easy way to enhance this technique for more pleasure.

1. Start by grabbing his penis and wrapping your fingers around the shaft. Your pinky finger should be closest to his balls while your index finger should be closest to the top of his penis.

2. Slowly stroke him up and down with your hand as you normally would.

3. This step is the important part: While stroking him up and down, rub your thumb over and back on the head of his penis. This means that your fingers will perform the standard up and down hand job technique, while your thumb is focused only on pleasuring the top of his penis.

4. Lube makes this technique much easier for you and far more satisfying for him.

7. Double Handed Backhand

The previous technique feels wonderful for your man, but it can be a bit tricky to master quickly. A much easier way to perform 'Traditional With A Twist' is to use both hands.

One hand will be focused on his shaft, jerking it up and down. The other will be focused on the head of his penis. Here are some hand job techniques you can use to stimulate the head and the tip.

• Keeping your fingers loose, run the tips of them over the head and then back again.

• Use the tip of one finger to make small circles around the tip of his penis.

• You can replace the hand that is stimulating the top of his penis with your tongue during a blow job. Your taste buds are slightly rough which means they provide massive amounts of stimulation without it ever being uncomfortable.

8. The Escalator

I call this technique 'The Escalator' because your hands never stop moving, just like an escalator never stops moving.

To start, you're going to take your right hand and stroke

him all the way from the top of his penis down to the bottom. Once your right hand reaches the bottom of his penis, take it away. You won't be stroking back upwards.

As your right hand reaches the bottom, take your left hand and perform the same motion, stroke him from the top of his penis all the way down to the bottom. When you reach the bottom of his penis, take your left hand away.

Now use your right hand again, and then your left, and then your right and so on. You will be doing this so that the moment your right hand reaches the bottom of his penis, you will then start stroking downwards with your left hand and so on.

This way, your man's penis will be feeling a constant stream of sensation from your hands. I highly recommend using lots of lube for this one.

Remember: The entire time, you will be stroking downwards only, from the tip of his penis to the base of his penis.

9. Balls In Play

In case you don't already know, your man's balls are insanely sensitive. So if you are just learning how to give a hand job, then you need to take advantage of this fact. This means that you can use one hand to give him a hand job, while at the same time using your free hand to massage his testicles. Here are some super erotic ways to do it.

Fondling – Fondling your man's balls is the easiest way to play with them. Cup them in your hands and play with them using your fingers. You should be super light here, allowing them to fall through your fingers and gently tickling them with your fingertips.

Pro Tip: Try this technique the next time you and your man shower together. Use a small amount of soap or shampoo on his balls for an extra silky feeling. You can also go further and learn how to have great shower sex.

Squeezing – Instead of just fondling his testicles, you can take them into your hand and softly squeeze them. The key word is 'softly.' If you are too hard or rough here, you may hurt your man and even injure him.

Pulling– This technique also requires caution, so you need to be gentle here. Otherwise, you may injure him. You need to gently grab your man's testicles and softly pull them away from his body. This doesn't provide that much stimulation during a hand job, but some guys adore this pulling technique as they climax and reach orgasm.

Licking/Sucking– This final testicle technique is more of a blow job technique. While giving him a handjob, you can take his balls into your mouth and softly lick, suck and massage them with your tongue. Of course, you need to careful not to hurt him or accidentally use your teeth here.

This technique can be crazy hot when your man is about to cum. Here's how it would work:

If he is standing, get down on your knees, like in this kneeling blow job position and take his balls into your mouth. Meanwhile, you should still be giving him a handjob. Then as he is cumming, he can give you a facial, depending on the position of his penis.

Doing this can feel a little awkward and be pretty tiring on your arms, so don't worry if you feel exhausted after less than a minute of doing this.

Milking & Sucking – An awesome way to suck your

man's balls while giving him a hand job is to have him get down on all fours so that when you are giving him a handjob, it looks like you are milking a cow. Seriously! The easiest way to give him a hand job (or milk him!) when he's on all fours is to position yourself behind him.

In this position, his balls will also be exposed, so it's perfect for sucking him. Take his balls into your mouth while using your hand(s) to milk him.

Also, you'll be in the perfect position to start eating his ass. Speaking of eating ass...

10. Anilingus HandJob

If you are just figuring out how to give a hand job to your man for the first time, then you may want to skip this next tip. It's called anilingus and as the name suggests, it involves pleasuring your man's butt.

You need to set your man up just like in the previous technique: he should be on all fours, and you should be behind him.

While giving your man a hand job, you are in the perfect position for anilingus. All you need to do is lick your man's anus and around it. You can also try licking his perineum in this position. Just make sure to check that it's clean first!

Go further with anal play. You can also learn:

• How to finger him anally

• How to give him a prostate massage

• How to use a strap on with your man

11. The Frenulum Is Your Friend

The most sensitive area on his penis is the head or glans; that's the purple part on the top of his penis. But the head of his penis covers a relatively large area, and you may be wondering what the most sensitive spot on the head is…

For almost all guys, the most sensitive spot on the head of their penis is the frenulum. This is the tiny piece of flesh on the underside of his penis that connects the shaft to the head, and it feels almost like a piece of string to the touch.

The most important piece of advice I can give you about the frenulum is to be gentle with it. If you apply intense pressure to it during a hand job, then it will probably feel painful for your man.

Instead, you need to be soft and gentle with it. Here are three hand job ideas to try on his frenulum

• Run your fingertips lightly over it.

• Softly flick it from side to side

• Stroke it up and down with just one finger.

An excellent hand job tip for finishing your man off is to start playing with his frenulum only when he is about to cum. This can make his orgasm feel very different when compared to a regular handjob.

Many men find that their frenulum is by far the most sensitive spot on their bodies. However, for some men, they don't find it particularly sensitive.

12. Twisting In Opposite Directions

Handjobs aren't just about stroking his cock up and down with a little variation here and there. You can also try twisting your hands around his cock instead of stroking it.

You may be wondering what the most pleasurable way to

twist your hands around his cock is...just follow these guidelines:

• Grab the bottom part of his shaft with one hand and grab the remaining part of his penis with your other hand so that both hands are holding it. Don't worry if your bottom hand is holding most of his penis and your other hand doesn't have much to hold.

• Without applying much pressure, rotate one hand in a clockwise direction around his penis while rotating your other hand in an anti-clockwise direction.

• When you can't turn either hand any further in one direction, change direction and rotate each hand as far as possible in the opposite direction.

• This sounds like quite a slow process, but it is much more pleasurable the faster you do it. Lube also helps you to speed it up without hurting your man.

NOTE: This can feel very much like giving your man an 'Indian burn' or 'Chinese burn' on his penis if you accidentally apply too much pressure and grab the skin of his penis. Doing this is excruciatingly painful for him.

So make sure that you use light enough pressure that your hands pass over the skin of his penis with ease without actually grabbing the skin. And remember, using plenty of lube makes this far, far easier and safer.

13. The Ring

The Ring is a very simple hand job technique to use if you are struggling to come up with new ideas. You just need to make an 'O' shape by touching the tip of your index finger to your thumb.

Then instead of wrapping your whole hand around your

man's shaft, use only the 'O' and then stroke him up and down with it.

When you combine The Ring with The Escalator technique that I mentioned above, it can feel both exhilarating for your man and very different to any other hand job technique.

14. Stroking Fast & Slow

When you masturbate by yourself, you may enjoy pleasuring yourself at various speeds. Sometimes you don't have time for a long, teasing build up and need to be fast. While on other occasions, you may have all the time in the world and take it slowly. Both can feel fantastic but are very different.

The same applies for your man. Giving him a quick hand job while he's standing in front of the mirror brushing his teeth in the morning can be super hot and very unexpected. It's going to feel very different to giving your man a massage and finishing it off with a slow, sensual hand job using lube.

This is the magic of changing up the speed of your hand jobs; you can provide your man with completely different sensations that still make him shake, shudder and scream as you make him cum.

Pro Tip: If you are trying out a new hand job technique on your man, try starting slowly. You'll find that it helps you master it faster.

15. Prostate Play

Many men adore having their prostate played with, and you're in the perfect position to massage his prostate when giving him a hand job.

To stimulate his prostate, you need to slide a finger inside his anus about 2-3 inches and then curl the tip backward towards his balls. The position of his prostate in his ass is similar to the position of your G Spot in your vagina.

You then need to stimulate it by stroking it, massaging it, pressing it and moving your finger in and out like you would when stimulating your G Spot.

If your man isn't used to anal play, then you need to take your time and make sure that your nails are trimmed. Using lube is very necessary, so make sure to have some nearby. If you want to try it in the spur of the moment, then saliva can be a good alternative.

16. Talking Dirty

Talking dirty to your man is not strictly a hand job technique, but it's a way to change things up and add yet another hyper pleasurable angle to your hand job toolbox.

While lying in bed together, try leaning over and start whispering some dirty talk in his ear while jerking him off. Talking dirty in this situation can be slightly tricky if you don't know what to say. Thankfully, there are two very easy things you can do.

1. Just tell him what you are doing, let him know how it feels and ask him for some feedback. Here's an example:

"I love feeling your cock in my hand and hearing you groan every time I stroke it. I can feel you precumming now and I'm going to rub it all over the tip of your cock. How does that feel? Do you want it faster or slower? I can't wait to feel you explode and cum everywhere for me."

This is much hotter if you softly whisper it in his ear

instead of saying it loudly.

2. Narrate a story for him as you jerk him off…making it about your hand job is even better! Here's an example:

"I'm that girl your mom warned you about. I just need to grab hold of your dick and then you're mine. I can stroke you fast or I can stroke you slow, it doesn't matter, because when your dick is in my hand, I control not only your orgasms, but I control you. And, I know you like it when I dominate you.

Now I want you to imagine all the hot, nasty, filthy things I could do to you as I jerk you off. It could be me whipping you, it could be me sitting on your face, it could be me tying you down in bondage and fucking you against your will or it could be me giving you this hand job."

17. Put On A Show For Me

If you aren't sure what technique your man enjoys most, then the best thing you can do is getting him to show you. Not only will you learn what he likes most, but you also get to see your man in complete ecstasy. As you lie down beside him and get him to jerk himself off, take note of:

• How he positions his hand(s).

• How fast or slow he jerks himself off.

• Does he hold his penis tightly or loosely?

• Does he speed up before he cums?

• Does he slow down or loosen his grip and he is cumming?

Once you know how he likes to get himself off, then it's time to steal his techniques so you can use them on him yourself.

Side note: You may also want to show him your favorite masturbation techniques, so he knows exactly what you like.

18. Lube Or No Lube

A nice way to increase the sensations when giving your man a 'handy' is to use some lube. You just need to have it close by when you start giving him a hand job and then add a little bit to your hands and his penis. This will make everything feel more slippery, sexy and luscious for both of you.

While you can certainly buy lube specifically for sex, you can just use coconut oil which is also edible. Do bear in mind that coconut oil does not play well with condoms and will degrade them quickly as it's oil based, so if you plan on moving on to sex after your hand job, make sure you use a water-based lube instead.

19. When Consistency Is Key

Many women (perhaps including you) find that a consistent rhythm during clitoral stimulation is best when you want to make yourself cum. If your man breaks this rhythm when rubbing your clit, it can be super frustrating.

Many guys feel the same when you are giving them a hand job (or blow job). As he gets closer and closer to orgasm, keeping a consistent rhythm is going to feel way more pleasurable than stopping and starting. So bear this in mind when your man is close to orgasm.

20. What Happens When He Reaches Orgasm

As your man reaches orgasm, you may be wondering,

"What do I do now?"

You only need to worry about two things here:

1. Where he shoots his load

2. How much pressure to apply

1. Where he shoots his load – This all depends on your preferences. If you enjoy it, you can let him ejaculate into your mouth and swallow his cum or spit it out. If you're naked, then you can allow him to ejaculate over your face, neck, breasts or any part of your body. You can also let him blow his load over your hands. Some people find this super hot; others don't. It all comes down to personal preference. Just be careful that it doesn't get into your vagina if you're not on the pill!

Alternatively, if you don't want his cum covering your body, you can let him ejaculate onto his own body or elsewhere.

2. How much pressure to apply – As your man starts to

ejaculate and shoot streams of semen from his penis, it may become super sensitive to touch. In this case, you should dramatically loosen your grip and slow down, so it's not painful for him.

Many women experience the same problem when climaxing; their clitoris becomes extra sensitive and even painful to touch. While not all guys experience this 'super-sensitivity,' most do.

21. Exciting New Locations

The easiest way to give your man a new hand job experience is to change the place where you jerk him off. Most couples reserve all their sexy times for the bedroom, but there are so many other great locations where you can totally blow your man's mind with your hand job skills.

• In the bathroom when he is getting ready for the day or just before bed.

• When you're both sitting down on the sofa together.

• Sneaking into a bathroom together at a party.

• While he's driving (just make sure not to break any laws!).

• Jumping in the shower with him after he's had a long day.

These are just a few examples. The key is doing some experimenting with new locations to see which you both find most exciting. If you like having sex outside, then try giving him a hand job outside.

22. Get Feedback

I've given you a huge bunch of different handjob tips, techniques, and ideas, but the crazy thing is that your man may only find a small fraction of them to be particularly enjoyable. You see, every guy is different and has different turn ons and techniques that he likes during a hand job.

While one guy may enjoy a particular technique, it may not be particularly satisfying for the next guy. So, you can spend lots of time trying to guess which technique he likes the most, but this is very haphazard, and you'll never be sure if he likes it or not.

The simple solution is to talk to him and get feedback on the techniques you are using. You don't need to interrogate him, but it is a good idea to ask him, "How does that feel?" or "Do you like that?" while trying a new technique or if you prefer, you can wait until after he has cum to ask him.

Even though this isn't necessarily a hand job technique

per se, I had to include it as many women (and men) never actually talk about this stuff and end up fumbling around for years, never sure if they truly satisfy their partner or not!

23. More, More, More....

Now that you know how to give a good hand job to your man (or any man), it's time to learn some more powerful sex techniques. With this in mind, you may have noticed is that it's very natural and easy to transition from a hand job to sucking his cock…you just need to get your mouth involved.

CHAPTER 4

COMMON HANDJOB MISTAKES WOMEN MAKE

You may remember fondly back to your high school days when your first contact with the male "parts" was giving your boyfriend a handjob. Back then, it was new and exciting and we had no idea what we were doing. But we remember it didn't last very long and he seemed to really enjoy it.

As we grew older and more sophisticated, you'd think that handjobs would lose their luster. They haven't, though, and they can be a really fun form of foreplay and anticipation. But as much as guys love those handjobs, that doesn't mean they can't be done better.

You probably don't feel like a hand job expert. While

this isn't exactly a core life skill, you obviously want to feel like you could give a hand job without fucking it up if you ever needed to. So fake some enthusiasm, remember that practice makes perfect, and avoid the following hand job mistakes at all costs.

1. Being Too Rough

I'm listing this as one mistake, but you should take many measures to avoid it. Incorporate lube/lotion/whatever moisturizing substance he has in his bedroom and used to hide when you came over. (This should be a given, but I'll say it anyway. You're trying to make him cum, not build a campfire. Friction is bad.)

If you have crazy long nails (especially acrylics), either wield with extreme caution or just hold off entirely. Remove all rings (for both your sakes). And please, please do not start whaling on it like you're trying to squeeze out the last of your toothpaste. Getting excited is great; forgetting that you're holding something with pain receptors is not.

2. Going On Autopilot

You may be tempted to pulling this whenever your man makes the slightest sound of encouragement. Once you know something's working, your immediate instinct is to repeat that exact move for the rest of your life. Unfortunately, you can't just check off "be good at sex" and never think about it again.

To consistently turn someone on, you need to be engaged in what you're doing and offer some variety. If a guy mechanically rubbed your clit like a broken marionette doll, you would be confused, frightened, and upset. Definitely take mental notes on what he's responding to, but remember that new sensations are often the most moan-worthy. (Especially if you've been using his "favorite move" to death).

Key elements to be switching up: the position of your hands (if you're feeling advanced, use both), the amount of pressure you apply, and your speed. (Speeding up when he's close is a good general rule, but careful not to ram your hand against the head. That shit is sensitive.)

3. Touching Only His Dick

While men often seem to delight in being reduced to their genitalia, hand jobs are an exception to that rule. If you stick to only touching his dick, you're severely limiting your options and risking both of you getting bored. Surprise ass play is never the move, so check in before trying that explicitly—but plenty other areas are available. Stroking his chest, playing with his balls, and rubbing behind his balls are all typically welcome additions to a hand job. It adds some much-needed variety, and has the added bonus of demonstrating how much you like touching him. As long as it's not causing him physical pain, all signs of enthusiasm/horniness are a major turn-on.

4. Not Giving A Personalized HandJob

We all know the core issue with handjobs: guys are always going to do this best themselves. To that end, the guy himself is your best source of information on how to give him a good hand job. If you're both comfortable with it, ask him to touch himself in front of you. When you take over, encourage him to tell you when he wants you to go harder/softer/faster/slower. Ask him if he likes his balls played with. Ask him where he's most sensitive and what to avoid. If you're uncomfortable having these conversations, that's what alcohol is for you can ease into it. Even a simple "does that feel good" goes a long way.

If you're on the opposite end of the spectrum, and highly confident in your technique, you should still check in with the guy. Every guy penis is different, and what worked for your ex could be totally off for another guy's taste. In most areas of life, communication is (sadly) key. Handjobs are no exception.

It's worth knowing that most guys I polled on this insisted there's no such thing as a good handjob. So while these tips should give you plenty to work with, don't let your hand job prowess ever stress you out. No guy will ever complain if you give up and switch to a blow job/sex/basically anything else sexual.

CHAPTER 5

FREQUENTLY ASKED QUESTIONS ABOUT

HANDJOBS

Have some pressing Qs before you get some handjob experience? We've got answers.

What do I do if there's foreskin?

Foreskin = a thin piece of skin that covers the head of the penis. Sometimes, a baby's parents decide to remove that flap — aka circumcise them.

If that skin is left intact, it can be retracted down the base of the penis, exposing the mushroom-like, oh-so-sensitive penis head beneath.

Some people will enjoy having their foreskin used as part of the hand job to add a layer of texture, warmth, and wetness. Other people might have a tighter foreskin, and it could be painful to try to retract their foreskin intentionally during a hand job.

To find out what your partner likes, ask!

How hard is too hard of a grip?

Generally, you want to start loose and increase grip as you go (up to a point, of course). But every penis owner prefers something different. So, grip your partner's cock, then ask:

• "Why don't you put your hand over mine and show me how tight you like it?"

• "Tell me when you like the tightness of my grip."

What do I do if my hand(s) gets tired?

Sex is supposed to be enjoyable for all partners. If finger fatigue is interfering with your pleasure, transition to another activity.

You might say:

• "Babe, I'm loving touching you, but my hand is getting tired. How would you feel about stroking yourself while I kiss your neck?"

• "How would you feel about me going down on you now?"

• "I think it could be really hot to watch you use a stroker on yourself."

What if I run out of spit?

Spit can be sexy, but it dries up pretty quickly and robs you of the slippery texture that makes stroking feel so good.

The solution? Use lube and be generous with it.

Why is my partner so quiet? Am I doing OK?

Moans aren't the only way to communicate how things feel. Changes in breath, body language, and facial expression can also offer some key clues.

Of course, if you're not sure whether they're enjoying themselves, there's one good way to find out how you're doing: Just ask! Ask simple questions like 'softer or harder?' or 'faster or slower?

What if there's pre-cum?

Pre-cum = pre-ejaculate that can dribble out of the tip of the penis anywhere from seconds to minutes before ejaculation. If your partner releases pre-cum, that's totally healthy and normal! Keep going (unless they ask you to stop, of course).

How to get things going?

Don't go from "hello" to handjob. Build arousal with:

• kissing

• massage

• dancing

• humping and grinding

• nipple stimulation

Finding a good position

Different muscles may bear more strain in different positions. Your hip and ab muscles will be more activated if you're straddling. Your shoulder muscles may feel strained if you're lying on your side, and each position may put different amounts of strain on your forearms. Do what's most comfortable for you and your partner.

Heating things up

No need to strip your boo to their birthday suit from the get-go. Tease them over their clothes by tracing the seams, outlining their penis through the fabric, or cupping your hand over their clothed cock and letting them grind into it.

When you're ready (and sense they're ready) for more, ask: "Can I take these off?"

How do I know if I should keep going?

If they're writhing or moaning like an (orgasmic) animal, they probs don't want you to stop. Keep doing what you're doing.

A quick "How does this feel?" or "Do you want me to keep going?" will clear up any confusion.

What about me!?

There are plenty of ways to get yours while giving a hand

job!

You could:

• Try a wearable sex toy like the b-vibe Rimming Plug or the We Vibe Moxie, both available online.

• Hump the mattress or your partner's thigh.

• Ask your partner to stimulate you at the same time.

• Use your other hand on yourself.

• Invite your partner to touch you when the hand job is done.

They're about to come... What do I do?

Keep going. You can either let them finish in your hand, ask them to finish themselves in their own hand, or grab a rag and use that to catch the cum. You could also let them finish in your mouth.

OK, they finished... Now what?

A little post-handy compliment goes a long way. Let your partner know how hot it was to watch them enjoy themselves.

Next, clean up. Then, if you want to be touched, let them know!

Conclusion

Sexual activity doesn't have to involve penetration to be satisfying, and hand sex isn't just teenage fodder. Hand jobs offer a lower-risk way to intimately connect with your partner without penetration.

You might choose to stop after the hand job, or maybe you favor them as sexy foreplay. Either way, your touch can still bring pleasure to your penis-owning partner (and you), no matter your age.

OTHER BOOKS BY THE AUTHOR

1. SUCK AND LICK HIM RIGHT: HOW TO GIVE GOOD HEAD AND BLOW HIM AWAY WITH HOT BLOW JOB TECHNIQUES

2. HOW TO TEASE, PLEASE AND GIVE HIM GREATEST SEX EVER: SUPER HOT LOVE MAKING TECHNIQUES TO PLEASURE AND SATISFY YOUR MAN IN BED SEXUALLY

3. ORAL SEX GUIDEBOOK FOR MEN: HOW TO EAT HER OUT AND GIVE HER BIG-O EVERY TIME

4. TALKING DIRTY TO YOUR MAN: SEXTINGS, PHONE TALKS AND WHAT TO SAY DURING SEX THAT WILL TURN HIM ON, PLEASE, TEASE AND DRIVE HIM CRAZY

5. HOW TO PLEASURE AND SATISFY YOUR MAN IN BED SEXUALLY: HOTTEST SEX TIPS EVERY WOMAN SHOULD FOLLOW

6. TALKING DIRTY TO YOUR WOMAN: SWEET SEXY THINGS YOU CAN SAY TO HER TO MAKE HER HORNY AND WET INSTANTLY

7. HOW TO GIVE HIM THE PERFECT BLOWJOB THAT WILL BLOW HIM AWAY: ORAL SEX IDEAS, TIPS, SKILLS, TECHNIQUES AND POSITIONS TO HELP YOU GIVE YOUR MAN

A MIND BLOWING, TOE-CURLING, ORGASMIC BJ

8. CUNNILINGUS (ORAL SEX) GUIDE TO GIVING HER MULTIPLE ORGASMS: MEN'S GUIDE TO GIVING HER GOOD HEAD THAT WILL MAKE HER SCREAM, MOAN, SHAKE, QUAKE AND SQUIRT

9. SUPER BLOWJOB TIPS, SECRETS, IDEAS, TECHNIQUES AND POSITIONS: HOW TO USE THEM TO TURN HIM ON, RIDE, TEASE, PLEASE, PLEASURE, SATISFY AND DRIVE YOUR MAN CRAZY IN BED (ORAL SEX GUIDEBOOK FOR WOMEN)

ALL AVAILABLE ON AMAZON AS E-BOOKS AND PAPERBACKS

Printed in Great Britain
by Amazon

37744496R00040